Forest Fire!

For Shirley
Special Thanks to Glen, Jill
and Kristin Mitchell

Published by Troll Communications L.L.C.

Published by arrangement with Fulcrum Publishing,
Golden, Colorado.

This edition published 1998.

Printed in the United States of America.

10 9 8 7 6 5 4 3 2 1

Library of Congress Cataloging-in-Publication Data

Fraser, Mary Ann.
    Forest fire! / by Mary Ann Fraser.
        p.   cm.
    Summary: Describes the forest life cycle and the destructive and renewing aspects of forest fire.
    ISBN 1-55591-251-6 (lib. bdg.) ISBN 0-8167-4962-0 (pbk.)
    1. Fire ecology—Juvenile literature. 2. Forest fires—Juvenile literature. 3. Forest ecology—Juvenile literature.
    [1. Fire ecology. 2. Forest fires. 3. Forest ecology. 4. Ecology.] I. Title.
    QH545.F5F735   1996
    574.5'2642—dc20   95-37035
                                                       CIP

Forest Fire!

Mary Ann Fraser

For two hundred fifty years debris had been collecting on the ancient forest floor. The entire valley was like a fire ring stacked with kindling.

High in the trees pine cones crackled in the heat of the afternoon. Below, a hungry bear and her cubs searched for berries and grubs. The noisy cubs startled an elk munching on a patch of withered grass nearby.

With the elk gone, a ground squirrel ventured from his burrow. Cautiously he scampered across the brown matted pine needles. Settling on a log, he sunned in one of the few shafts of light that found its way through the dense tree branches.

Suddenly a gust of wind ripped through the trees. There was a sound of splintering wood. The ground squirrel leaped out of the way just as a lodgepole pine, killed by bark beetles, fell to the ground. CRASH!

There was a hush over the valley. Clouds, like steam from a boiling cauldron, rolled over the mountain peaks. Thunder broke the silence. The elk lifted his head to the sky. The bear sniffed the air. The ground squirrel peeked out from a hollowed stump.

There was a blinding flash and then BOOM! CRACK! Lightning struck the top of an old, dead pine. The tree burst into flames. The crackling blaze spread from treetop to treetop like the lighting of torches. Sparks rained onto the brittle pine needles and raced across the forest floor. Soon the entire valley was engulfed in flames and whipped into a firestorm by the strong winds.

Boulders exploded from the heat. Smoke inked out the sun. Wind roared through the area like a freight train. The wide-eyed elk bounded past the bear family, who stumbled and rolled their way to a hollow by the creek. The ground squirrel darted into his burrow to escape the flames that raced toward him.

For months pockets of fire smoldered in the roots and stumps of trees. At last an autumn rain snuffed out the last remaining embers. The narrow valley, once covered by old-growth trees, had quickly become a charred and barren landscape.

But the forest had not died.

Many of the cones of the lodgepole pines had a resin coating to protect them. The fire had melted the resin. Now these cones sprung open and scattered their seeds. The ground squirrel ate some of these pine seeds and buried others to eat later. Some he never found again. These forgotten seeds would be ready to sprout in the coming spring.

Although most of the bushes had been burned, those with deep roots were still alive. Within weeks they had new shoots poking up among their blackened branches. The elk nibbled at the new stems and leaves and licked the ash for its minerals. Like all of the forest animals, he needed to build thick layers of fat to survive the difficult winter.

The ground squirrel and the bears began their long
hibernation just before a fierce blizzard draped the valley
in snow. An old mule deer who had survived the fire now
died from the cold. He became food for a starving coyote.

Spring was a time of renewal for the valley. Snowmelt seeped through the ash and carried nutrients for plants into the soil and streams. Since treetops no longer blocked the sun, the lodgepole pine seeds sprouted in the warm, moist earth. Mushrooms popped up beside the rotting, burnt timber and helped break it down, enriching the soil. The bear family awoke from their winter hibernation and feasted on the animals that had died during the winter.

Grass seeds carried by the wind burst forth into a lush carpet patterned by wildflowers of every color. Wood beetles, millipedes, mites and ant colonies had escaped the fire by hiding under rocks or below ground. As the seedlings sprang up, many above-ground insects, which had flown away, returned. The new plants gave them food and places to hide and lay their eggs. Deer and elk grew fat on the grasses, which contained more nutrients than grasses growing in unburned areas.

More bats and birds than ever before came to the valley to feed on the many insects. As the woodpeckers drilled holes into the burned-out trees looking for bark beetle larvae, they created nesting sites for songbirds.

Mice, chipmunks and squirrels had bulging cheeks from all the seeds they gathered. Soon owls, snakes, foxes, coyotes and weasels came to raise their families and to hunt these small rodents.

After five years the pine seedlings were only one to two feet high. When strong winds blew, burned trees toppled into the creek and calmed its rushing currents. The fallen timber together with minerals washed into the sun-bathed stream created perfect conditions for water plants and algae to grow. Water insects such as mayflies, caddis flies and stone flies ate these plants. They became food for the trout.

The mother bear spent many late afternoons alone catching fish, since her cubs had left to find their own territories. A moose gave birth to her calf among some willows. The valley once again could provide food and shelter for many kinds of creatures. The fire had renewed the forest.

After twenty-five years the valley supported more plants and animals than the earlier old forest. Ground squirrels darted and zigzagged through sagebrush. Elk, deer, moose and bison grazed in the open fields surrounded by young fir and spruce, aspen and pine.

Over the next two hundred years the sun-loving grasses, wildflowers and shrubs died as the trees' interwoven branches blocked the sun. Many deer and bison left to find better grazing, but animals like the goshawk, which depend on old-growth forests, moved in. The valley had come full circle. Someday, when conditions are just right, a tiny spark will begin the forest's life cycle once again.